Fun Group Games for Children's Ministry

Loveland, Colorado

Fun Group Games for Children's Ministry
Copyright © 1990 by Group Publishing, Inc.

Second Printing, 1991

Credits
Edited by Lee Sparks
Cover designed by Jill Bendykowski
Cover photo by David Priest and Brenda Rundback
Interior designed by Judy Atwood Bienick
Illustrations by Mary Lynn Ulrich

Scripture quotations are from the Holy Bible, New International Version. Copyright © 1973, 1978, 1984 International Bible Society. Used by permission of Zondervan Bible Publishers.

Library of Congress Cataloging-in-Publication Data
Fun group games for children's ministry.
    p.   cm.
    ISBN 1-55945-003-7
    1. Games in Christian education. 2. Church work with children. 3. Games.
4. Bible games and puzzles. I. Group Books (Firm)
BV1536.3.F85 1990
268'.432—dc20   90-34804
                                                                  CIP

Printed in the United States of America

CONTRIBUTORS

The editors of Group Books thank the writers who contributed to this collection. The editors are confident that their idea-sharing will enhance your ministry with children. The contributors:

Karen Ball
Sandi Black
Brian Cress
Carol Davant
Cindy Hansen
Margaret Hinchey
Delores Johnson
Janel Kauffman
Dawn Korth

Paul Lippard
Jolene Roehlkepartain
Louisa Rogers
Linda Snyder
Norman Stolpe
Terry Vermillion
Brett Younger
Carol Younger
Chris Yount

CONTENTS

Teamwork Builders

Games With a Message

Bible-Learning Games

Energy Burners

Group Fun

Relays

INTRODUCTION

Children love to play. And many child-development experts claim that children need to play more often these days. In our culture of the "hurried child," in which many forces are accused of pushing a child to grow up faster than he or she should, perhaps the ministry of play is one of the more valuable ministries of the church. And adults, if they're honest with themselves, will probably admit a degree of jealousy that children get to play more often than adults do.

In *Fun Group Games for Children's Ministry*, Group has collected 100 active, creative activities for children. There are games for increasing Bible knowledge, building community, enhancing teamwork, getting acquainted, running relays and simply burning excess energy. Use these games to introduce or amplify whatever message or point you want children to deal with.

No children's ministry should be all "fun 'n' games," but every one should have some element of fun to meet kids' needs. Games alone can't be the focus of ministry with children—but they remain an essential ingredient. Enjoy these games and the fun you'll provide for the children you minister to.

PART 1

·····················

Getting-to-Know-You-Games

❋*B*ackward Autographs

This is a fast-paced mixer or get-acquainted game.

You'll need a pencil and a piece of paper for each child.

Give children exactly three minutes (or more if it's a large group) to exchange autographs with as many others as they can. But each child must write his or her name backward. At the end of the time, the child who's collected the most signatures—and can identify whose they are—is the winner.

❄*B*op on the Head

This is a great way to help children get to know one another's names.

You'll need enough chairs for the number of children in the group—minus one. You'll also need a "bat." The bat can be made from a wrapping-paper tube or from rolled newspapers. Or use a Nerf-type bat. Make sure the bat is soft.

Have children sit in a circle on chairs. Give one child the bat and send him or her to the center.

Have one seated child start the game by saying his or her name and the name of someone else in the group. The person in the center then tries to "bop" on the head the second person named—before that person says his or her name and another person's name.

Any person who's bopped before he or she can say the second name then goes in the center to take the bat. The former child in the center sits down and starts the cycle over again by saying his or her name and the name of another child.

★Draw Your Neighbor

This activity helps children get acquainted and have fun drawing.

You'll need slips of paper, a hat or basket, blank pieces of paper for drawing and pencils. Different-color pencils or markers can be used if desired. You'll also need tape or thumbtacks.

Have children each write their name on a slip of paper. Gather all the names in a hat or basket. Ask children to each draw a name but not to look at the person whose name they've picked. They're to keep the names they picked a secret. After everyone picks a name, have children each draw a picture of the person whose name they picked, without letting anyone see. Allow about 10 minutes for drawing. Instruct children each to draw just the face of the person they picked. When they're finished, have children place the drawings in the middle of the floor, face down.

When all the drawings are in, shuffle them for added suspense and then tape or tack them to a wall. Have children guess who each drawing represents and who drew the picture.

Drawings can be left on the wall or taped together to form a group portrait.

❀ *Four Corners*

This active game helps kids learn new things about each other. As you stand in the middle of the room and call out the choices below, point to a corner for each choice. Have children each move to the corner that best fits them. Ask children to talk with the rest of the children in that corner about why they chose that corner. If time allows, call on someone from each corner to share what attracted kids to that corner.

The following are some sample categories.

My favorite food is:

● hamburgers (point to corner #1)

● pizza (point to corner #2)

● steak (point to corner #3)

● seafood (point to corner #4)

My favorite vacation is:

● going to Disneyland (point to corner #1)

● skiing (point to corner #2)

● swimming at the beach (point to corner #3)

● visiting relatives (point to corner #4)

My favorite room in the house is:

● the kitchen (point to corner #1)

● the family room (point to corner #2)

● my bedroom (point to corner #3)

● the bathroom (point to corner #4)

Other options: spectator sports, participatory sports, school subjects, games or TV shows. Pick things that interest your group.

✳*Friend* Acrostic

This non-competitive activity helps children reveal facts about themselves.

For each child, you'll need a pencil and a piece of paper with a word or phrase spelled out vertically down the left margin. You can use the name of your group, a greeting or any appropriate word or phrase that has fewer total letters than the number of participants.

Have each child go to other children and get them each to write something about themselves that starts with a letter in the vertical word or phrase. Here's an example:

*H*as three sisters
*E*lephants—She collects them.
*L*oves music
*L*ong hair
*O*rdinarily skips breakfast

The first person who gets his or her acrostic completely filled out and can match each fact with the appropriate child is the winner.

✸*G*reat Impressions

This non-threatening activity helps children associate themselves with things around them.

You'll need enough clay, Silly Putty or Play-Doh for each person to have a small piece.

Give each child a piece of clay, Silly Putty or Play-Doh. Then ask children each to leave the room and make an impression on the clay of something in the church. For example, the tread from the bottom of the pastor's shoe, the words on the cover of a Bible, or a heating vent. Then have children take turns showing their impressions to the group while others guess what they are. After each correct guess, have the child who made that impression explain why he or she chose that item.

❄*L ist Game*

This activity helps children discover things they have in common.

You'll need a large piece of posterboard and markers. For each child, you'll need a pencil and a piece of paper numbered from one to 10.

Use the posterboard and markers to create a numbered list of 10 things that children have in common. Place the list where everyone can see it. Give each child a pencil and piece of paper numbered from one to 10. On "go," have the children each find someone who fits the description of one of the numbered items. Have the "discovered" child sign the other child's paper next to the appropriate number. If your group is large, make a rule that there can be no repeats. The list might read:

1. Someone who uses the same color toothbrush as you do.

2. Someone who has the same last digit in his or her phone number as you do.

3. Someone who has the same shoe size as you do.

4. Someone who was born in the same state as you were.

5. Someone who has the same number of brothers and sisters as you do.

6. Someone who was born in the same month as you were.

7. Someone whose family has the same kind of car as your family does.

8. Someone who had the same thing for breakfast as you did.

9. Someone who has the same favorite food as you do.

10. Someone who goes to the same dentist as you do.

The winner is the person who fills his or her paper first.

★*M*ap Your Life

This is a non-threatening activity that helps children share where they were born and where they've visited or would like to visit.

You'll need a big map of North America, or better yet, the world. You'll also need a few markers.

Post the map on the wall in your meeting room. Have children each mark the following three spots with their initials:

- where they were born;
- one place they've visited; and
- one place they hope to visit someday.

After children each have marked their three spots, point to each spot and have the child whose initials are there tell why he or she chose that place.

❀ *Meetin' Meetings*

This fast-paced game encourages kids to share about themselves. For each team you'll need a lightweight object that can be tossed onto laps such as a Nerf ball or handkerchief.

Form teams of three or four. Give each team a Nerf ball, handkerchief or any lightweight object that can be tossed onto laps. Have the person with the longest fingers start.

The first player tosses the object onto a teammate's lap while everyone claps slowly in unison. As the object is tossed, he or she calls out one of four categories:

● family;
● friends;
● room; or
● school.

The receiver must catch the object, then call out an object or person in his or her life that fits that category. For example, if "friends" is called out, the receiver might say "John." The receiver must call out an answer within two claps. Then it's his or her turn to toss the object. If a receiver fails, possession returns to the player who tossed the object.

Allow three to five minutes. Then have each team's players say their own names. Then have their teammates tell all they learned about each child. For example, "Katie has a desk in her room." Give each piece of information 1 point.

After all children have been introduced, the team with the most points wins.

✳*N*ame Game

All you need is an old sock filled with cotton and tied closed to help children learn each other's names.

Have children sit in a circle. Designate one person to be "It." He or she sits in the middle armed with the cotton-filled sock. One child starts by saying someone else's name in the circle. The child named must then name another child in the circle before getting walloped with the flying sock.

When a child gets hit with the sock, he or she becomes the new "It." The former "It" joins the circle and starts a new round by calling out a name. If "It" throws the sock after the child has said a name, "It" stays in the middle.

✳*P*eople Place Mats

This activity works well on its own but is especially effective when used with a group snack or meal.

For each child, you'll need a marker and an inexpensive white paper place mat.

Place the markers and place mats around on tables. As children come in, have each one sit in front of a place mat. Ask the kids each to divide their place mat into four sections with the marker. Have children each number the corners and use their best creative ability to describe the following things:

Square 1—Draw a symbol that represents your family when they're together.

Square 2—Draw a symbol of what you want to be when you're older.

Square 3—Draw a picture of what you enjoy most with your friends.

Square 4—Draw a picture of your favorite Christmas or other holiday.

Have children each share their drawings with four children around them or with the whole group, depending on the size of the group.

❄ *P*uzzle Partners

This get-acquainted activity can be used to divide kids into pairs or smaller groups.

You'll need pictures cut from magazines, and if you wish, copies of the discussion-starters below.

Cut out magazine pictures that show people involved in various activities. Cut each picture into two or more pieces.

Give each child a piece of a picture. Have children mill around and find out who has other pieces of their pictures. Then have each pair or small group with the same picture sit together, assemble the picture and talk together. Some discussion-starters:

● How are you like someone in the picture?

● If you were in the scene pictured, what would you be doing? saying?

● What incident in your life does the picture remind you of?

● If a member of your family saw you doing what's pictured, what would he or she say?

● Where would you rather be—in the picture or in math class? Why?

For a variation on the game, have pairs or small groups each create a caption for their picture. Then have the large group choose the most creative caption as the winner. Or have pairs or small groups create skits based on their pictures to perform for everyone else.

★ Read and Match

Before the meeting collect subscription cards from various magazines. You'll need two cards from each magazine. Scramble the cards.

When children arrive, give each child one card. Have children each search for another child who has a card from the same magazine without saying the name of their magazine. Instead, children each must ask yes-or-no questions about the magazine, such as: "Does your magazine deal with animals?" or "Is your magazine for adults?"

When children find their partners, have pairs choose which of the two cards grabs their attention more. Then have the child who's holding that card say what he or she enjoys reading and why. Then have the partner do the same.

❀ Which Are You Like?

This activity helps children develop a sense of themselves and others.

Before the meeting, create a series of pairs of related but contrasting items, such as "breakfast/dinner" or "winter/summer." Some examples:

a couch or a rocking chair
green or yellow
water or Earth
pizza or ice cream
a freeway or a country road
an onion or an apple
north or south
a candle or a flashlight
a kite or a Frisbee

a TV show or a book
plastic or wood
an attic or a basement
a folk song or a popular hit
a bath or a shower
Saturday or Wednesday
corduroy or denim

Have children mingle in a large, open space. Then call out one pair of items, using the question, "Are you more like____ or____?" Have children go to one side of the room if they feel like one item or the other side of the room if they feel like the opposite item. No in-betweeners allowed!

Randomly select children from each side of the room. Ask each child to explain why he or she feels more like one item than the other. After three or four kids have contributed, have the group return to the middle of the room to start on the next pair of items. Repeat the game as long as you wish.

PART 2

···

Teamwork
Builders

✳ **A**rt in the Dark

Teams compete in this indoor drawing game. It'll take 10 to 30 minutes, depending on the number of drawings you choose to do.

You'll need a very dark room. For each team, you'll need a pencil, a pad of paper and slips of paper with words for players to illustrate.

This game is like other drawing games: a member of each team is given a word and must draw a picture that'll help other team members guess it. The difference is that each child must draw the picture in the dark.

Form teams of no more thán five. With the lights on, call a member of each team forward. Show him or her a slip of paper on which you've written a word like one of those below. Allow the players to return to their teams and pick up a pencil and pad of paper. Then turn the lights out. Give the players 30 to 45 seconds of darkness in which to draw, then shout "Stop" and turn on the lights. If you can't fully darken a room or want to keep the lights on, a variation can be to blindfold each artist.

The player shows his or her picture to other members of the team, who begin to call out guesses. The first team to correctly identify the word gets one point, and the team with the most points wins.

Some suggestions for words to use: socks, garden, pineapple, cactus, ski, basketball, mother, tornado, scissors, caterpillar, kick, camel, toenail, diaper, notebook, smoke, yawn, cook, zebra, wheelchair, stop, puzzle, bus, clown, smile, cry, pretzel.

✸*Beanbag Volley*

Volleyball, often the highlight of church picnics, is also popular among kids. Try this wild variation.

You'll need a volleyball net, four to six beanbags and a whistle.

Divide the group into two teams, with one team on each side of the net. Give each team two or three beanbags. The more beanbags, the crazier the game.

At the sound of the whistle, the beanbags are tossed over the net to the opposing team. The opposing team tries to catch the beanbags.

After a beanbag is caught, it's tossed back over the net. If the beanbag is not caught, it's picked up and tossed over the net. The less time between tosses, the better the game.

One point is scored for each beanbag a team catches. The first team scoring 5 points wins the game. The game is then restarted with an equal number of beanbags on both sides. The first team to win three games wins the match.

❄*Burst a Bubble*

This game gives kids a chance to burn energy and have fun.

You'll need two jars of bubble mixture. Buy these in grocery or discount stores, or make your own by mixing one part liquid Ivory soap with two parts water. Empty thread spools can be used as bubble-blowers. Bring bubble gum for prizes.

Have kids number off using "bubble" or "burst" instead of numbers. Then have all "bubbles" form one team and all "bursts" form another.

Give one person on each team a jar of bubble mixture. Have that person be the team's bubble-blower. Also, have one person on each team try to pop as many bubbles as he or she can. Have the other team members count the number of burst bubbles. On "go," have the bubble-blowers blow bubbles. Change bubble-blowers and bubble-poppers after one minute. Continue until each team member has played.

Ask the teams to add their total number of burst bubbles. Award two pieces of bubble gum to each winning team member. Give the other team members each one piece for a job well-done.

✯ Crab Soccer

This game follows the basic rules of soccer, except kids play indoors. And it's less competitive since all players are "crabs." Even non-athletic kids enjoy this game, and everyone gets a good laugh.

You'll need a soccer ball. Set up goals like soccer, only smaller.

Form two teams and play soccer. But have all players walk and kick the ball like crabs—with their bellies in the air and walking on all fours. Encourage teams to "strategize" just like they would in soccer.

❀ Don't Melt the Ice

This activity helps kids learn about sharing and working together. You'll need a supply of equal-size ice cubes.

Form two teams. Have teams each stand in a circle, facing inward. Give each team an ice cube.

At the signal, teams pass the ice cube around like a "hot potato." If the ice cube is dropped, a five-second "holding" penalty is enforced. The ice cube is held tightly in the hand of the person who dropped it.

The last team with a bit of ice remaining wins.

✳ *H*olly-Jolly Obstacle Course

This game can be used during Christmas season. It burns off lots of energy.

You'll need inflated inner tubes, straw or hay, scarves, hats, mittens, songbooks, tree branches, tinsel, ornaments, ice water, tubs, green hats, hammers, boards, nails, red hats, toys, bags, crowns, boxes of "jewels," housecoats and towels.

Before the group arrives, set up the course for two teams in two separate lines.

Form two teams. Each team sends one person at a time through the series of activities. The object is to be the first team to get every team member through the course.

At each activity the child completes a task relating to Christmas:

● **Manger**—Put straw or hay in the middle of an inner tube and then sit in it.

● **Caroler**—Put on a scarf, hat, and mittens, and pick up a songbook and sing "Joy to the World!"

● **Christmas Tree**—Decorate a tree branch with an ornament and five pieces of tinsel.

● **Chilly Water**—Walk through a tub of ice water.

● **Elf**—Put on a green hat and hammer a nail into a board.

● **Santa**—Put on a red hat, put toys in a bag and say, "Ho, Ho, Ho."

● **Wiseman**—Put on a crown, pick up a box of jewels, and say, "Follow that star!"

● **Shepherd**—Put on a housecoat, place a towel on your head and look for your sheep.

✳*M*acaroni Messages

This word game can be used for individual, partner or team competition.

You'll need approximately one box of dry alphabet macaroni for every four to six players.

Spill the macaroni on a table in front of the players where everyone can reach it. Then call out clues like the ones below. Players grab for letters and spell out words in front of them. Pairs or teams can work together.

The first person, pair or team to form a word earns a point, and the team with the most points after a set time wins.

Some clues: a circus animal, a name of a car, a kind of soap, something a firefighter uses, what a baby does, a day of the week, a subject studied in school, a name of a department store, a sport, a cartoon character, an article of clothing, an ice cream flavor, a name of a big city, a vegetable, a fast-food restaurant.

❄*M*itten Menace

This game helps "equalize" the skills of coordinated and not-so-coordinated kids so all can compete.

For each team, you'll need a pair of mittens, a paper bag, some unshelled peanuts and yarn.

Form two equal teams. Have teams each form a circle. Give each team a pair of mittens, and a paper bag with a peanut for each team member. Tie each paper bag shut with a piece of yarn.

On "go," have one child on each team put on the mittens and untie the bag. With the mittens still on, have the person pull out one peanut, shell it, eat it and retie the yarn around the bag. Then have him or her pass the mittens and bag to the person on his or her left. Have teams continue until everyone has participated.

The first team to finish wins.

Variation: Instead of unshelled peanuts use fortune cookies and have each person read his or her fortune aloud after eating the cookie.

☆*Musical* Instruments

Form teams of two to 10 players. Have each group move into its own space (different rooms, if possible) and —without any props or materials—create a musical instrument complete with sound and movement. Give groups exactly five minutes. Then have groups each perform their instrument. Re-form different groups and play again.

✿*One-Handed* Art

This non-competitive activity for partners requires children to work together.

You'll need art supplies such as modeling clay, construction paper, glue, string, crayons, markers or paint. A wide variety of materials is nice but not required.

Form pairs. Instruct partners each to work together to create something using materials of their choice. But each partner can use only one hand. Right-handers must each use their left hand and left-handers must each use their right hand. Both partners must contribute to the creation.

Competition is not required. If you wish, winners could be the pair with the most attractive or creative finished product.

✽*P*eople Scramble

This game requires kids to think and act quickly to spell words.

You'll need markers, tape and a few pieces of paper. Form two teams. Ask an adult volunteer to be the scribe for each team.

Tape a piece of paper with one letter of the alphabet on the front of each teammate. For example, if you have five players on each team, use letters such as R, S, T, N and A. Add letters if you have more players. Each child should get a different letter. Each team should get a different set of letters to encourage creativity. Be sure each team has a vowel or two.

On "go," have children scramble and rearrange themselves to spell as many words as they can think of using as many of the players as they wish. Have the scribe write the words formed by the players. For example, using the letters above the kids could spell: at, tar, as, rat, star, tan, Stan, an, ran and sat.

After five minutes, stop to see which team has created the most words.

❋ Pingpong Blow

Got any windbags in your group? Here's a game that'll blow off a lot of steam.

You'll need several pingpong balls and some masking tape.

Form two teams. Have teams kneel on opposite sides of a large table. Put a line of masking tape down the middle of the table between the two teams.

Have all team members clasp their hands behind their backs. Have players try to blow pingpong balls across the table to fall off the table on the opponent's side.

Start with one pingpong ball, but gradually add more until you have about seven balls going at once. The team to get the most pingpong balls blown off the opponent's side within five minutes wins.

❄**P**uzzle Trade

This game is a fun, competitive teamwork-builder game for any number of small teams.

For each team, you'll need a large picture or poster, a plastic bag and several pairs of scissors.

Form teams of three. Give teams each a different picture or poster, and have them cut their picture apart to create a jigsaw puzzle. Have teams each keep their picture a secret and make the puzzle as difficult as possible. Explain that they'll be exchanging puzzles with another team. No puzzle piece may be smaller than one square inch. You might also want to set a limit on the number of puzzle pieces. Give the teams a few minutes to create the puzzles, but don't rush them.

After teams each have completed their puzzle, instruct them to put the puzzle pieces in a plastic bag. Place all the puzzles in a pile. Have each team choose a runner.

On "go," have the runners each dash to the pile, grab a puzzle that's not their team's, and take it back to their team to be assembled. The first team to correctly assemble a puzzle wins.

★**P**yramid Races

No doubt you've seen or been in a human pyramid. But this game adds another dimension to human pyramids; they move.

Form teams of three. Designate a turn-around point about 20 feet away. Have two children from each team get down on their hands and knees side by side. Have the third child kneel on top of the two kneeling teammates. Be sure the child on top isn't too heavy for the kids below.

Race to see which team can crawl to the designated point and back first without the top person falling off.

❀ Questionable Football

This game is a good activity anytime, but especially so in the fall when football commands so much attention.

Form two teams. Each team huddles and chooses an object for their opponents to guess. The object doesn't need to be in the room. Line up the two teams facing each other, with several feet between them. Using masking tape, mark one-foot lines between the teams, to look somewhat like a football gridiron. Toss a coin to decide who "kicks off."

The player on the far right of the line begins by asking the player facing him or her a yes-or-no question about the object. A "yes" wins a "first down." The team keeps possession. The next teammate asks a question. A "no" causes a "turnover." Play continues using the rules below until one team scores a "touchdown."

● **First Down**—When the team takes one step forward to the next line after a "yes."

● **Forward Pass**—When a player makes a correct guess on the object before the team has crossed the goal line. This scores a touchdown.

● **Fumble**—When a player makes an incorrect guess on a forward pass. The entire team must return to the starting line-up.

● **Turnover**—When possession passes to the rival team after a "no."

● **Huddle**—Time out. Two per team allowed to plan strategy and questions to ask.

● **Touchdown**—Wins the game. Can be achieved through either a forward pass or a series of first downs. When the entire team crosses the goal line, the team must make a guess. If the team guess correctly, it wins. If not, the entire team returns to the starting line-up.

✳ *R*acing Dr. Seuss

Who'd have thought a book by Dr. Seuss could be used to teach about teamwork?

You'll need a Dr. Seuss book with approximately the same number of pages for each team. Possibilities include: *The Cat in the Hat, Hop on Pop, How the Grinch Stole Christmas, The Butter Battle Book* or *Don and Donna Go to Bat.*

Form teams of four or five. Give each team a Dr. Seuss book. Have the children sit in a circle. Have each child read a page of the book aloud and act out an action on that page. If there are no verbs, have children imitate sounds, characters or silly nouns on the page. Then have that child pass the book to the next child who reads the next page and does the same thing.

The first team to finish its book wins.

✳ *S*nake

Have kids make a human snake and have a lot of fun. You don't need any materials, just add kids.

Form at least two teams. Have the teams gather behind a starting line. The object is to make a human snake that stretches around the room, gym, or hallway, around a goal and back to the starting line. The longer the course, the better.

On "go," the first child on each team lies on the ground with his or her hands on the starting line and feet stretched down-field. As soon as the first child is lying down, the second child runs and grabs the feet of the first child and lies down. As soon as the second child is lying down, the third child grabs the second child's feet and lies down, and so on.

When everyone in line is lying down as part of the snake, have the first person get up, run to the end of the

snake and hook on again. Then have children continue
the action until the team completes the course.

It's best to have an adult at the head of each line to tell
each child when he or she can run to the end of the
snake.

❄ *Solve a Mystery*

Children love mysteries, especially Nancy Drew and the Hardy Boys. Here's a game that lets kids be super sleuths and compete with each other.

You'll need some 3×5 cards and pencils.

You supply the crime and clues for this game. Choose an "unsolved mystery" for your group. For example: Someone left the church lights on for three days. Give each group member a 3×5 card with one clue on it. Clues should include the time the crime happened, where the crime happened, the people present just before the crime occurred, the first or last letter of the criminal's name and who reported the crime. Have children put all their information together and make a list of suspects and questions to ask them.

When the group asks to question a suspect, provide one by having someone play the part. You may take on the suspect role yourself and provide any information children need. Each child may ask one question of each suspect.

When your time is over for questioning, have each child use the blank side of his or her 3×5 card to write down who's guilty. Let the children compare their answers and decide on one culprit. Then give them the correct answer in Perry Mason style, by going back to the scene of the crime and replaying what happened.

✫ *Stringing Macaroni*

This is a good community-building game.

You'll need a 5-foot length of string and a box of uncooked elbow macaroni for each team.

Form teams of four to seven people. Have the teams each line up behind a line. Hand the first child on each team the string (with a large knot tied in one end) and the macaroni. At a signal, the first person strings one macaroni and runs it to the other end of the string. As soon as the macaroni is at the end of the string, the next person may start. The first team to fill the string with macaroni wins.

Kids will need to cooperate to continuously string macaroni.

❀ Super Sniffers

This game's nothing to sneeze at.

You'll need a dozen spices, such as oregano, basil, thyme, chili powder, dill, garlic and turmeric. Put 1/4 teaspoon of each spice or herb into four different paper bags. Number each bag and tie it shut with a piece of yarn so kids can't see inside.

Form two teams. Give each team a set of bags, including two bags of each spice. Spread the bags out on a table for each team. Have teammates work together to match a bag of one smell with another bag of the same smell. Don't allow kids to shuffle bags. After five minutes, see how many correct matches each team has.

✳ *Team* Crossword

This is a large-scale team game that requires children to work well with one another to win.

For each team, you'll need 50 pieces of paper with a letter of the alphabet printed on each one. You'll also need a sheet of clues for each team.

Give each team these 50 letters:

6: E

5 each: A I O

3 each: R N T U

2 each: L M S Z

1 each: B C D F H K P W Y

On the floor or ground have each team create a giant crossword puzzle forming words from clues you give them. Some clues to use: where you spend most of your time, name of your favorite food, what you want for your birthday, something you read, a musical instrument, a kind of pet, a month of the year, a toy you once played with, your favorite color, something with stripes.

Score 1 point for each letter used. It's not absolutely necessary for words to intersect, but each word that successfully intersects another word earns an additional 5 points.

After three or four clues, teams may run out of the letters they need. The game ends when teams can no longer play. The highest score wins.

❋ Team Frisbee

This game forces partners to work together while they play Frisbee. For each four children you'll need a Frisbee.

Have two sets of partners play Frisbee. But the partners' arms must be linked at all times. Or the partners' legs must be tied together with bandannas or ties.

❄ Watch the Earth Move

For this game, have children take off their shoes. You'll need a beach ball.

Form a long line. Have children lie on their backs with their heads all pointing the same direction. Then—using only hands and feet—have kids pass the "Earth" from one end of the line to the other.

When one player passes the Earth, have him or her jump up and run to the end of the line to keep the Earth moving. Play until you run out of room or until everyone has passed the Earth several times.

PART 3
Games With a Message

★*Arthritic Hands*

This game helps children experience having physical limitations.

For every two children, you'll need an elastic bandage, a glass of water, a newspaper and a buttoned jacket or sweater.

Form pairs. Have one partner from each pair wrap up the other's hands in elastic bandages so he or she can't use any fingers. Have the "handicapped" children each complete the following exercises:

● Drink a glass of water;

● Page through a newspaper; and

● Put on a buttoned jacket or sweater and button all the buttons.

Then switch roles so the other partner can experience the same.

❀ Blind Times

This game helps children understand how it feels to be blind.

You'll need two blindfolds, a glass of water, paper and pencils. Form two teams of equal size.

One at a time, have children from each team come forward to a table. Blindfold one child from each team. Then have teammates cheer as the two blindfolded children each do these tasks:

● Pour water into a glass.

● Write their name on a piece of paper.

● Walk back to the team to tag the next teammate to come forward.

After the game, talk about how it felt not to be able to see while trying to do the tasks.

✳ Dodging Drugs

This game is a great warm-up activity for a meeting about drug abuse. You'll need a small ball of yarn (1 to 2 feet of yarn) for each child and some handkerchiefs for this game.

Form two teams. Give each child a ball of yarn. Tell children to try to hit someone on the other team with the ball of yarn on the count of three. Ask kids to pay attention to where they're hit with other balls of yarn. Then, on the count of three—let 'em at it!

After the balls of yarn have been thrown, have players each unroll the ball(s) that hit them and tie the yarn to the body part hit. If the head was hit, have children use the handkerchiefs to cover the closest feature (eyes, mouth or ears). Not all players will be hit.

Children may not use the body part(s) marked with the yarn or handkerchiefs in any activity for the rest of the session. For example, those with arms marked can't write or catch, and those with blindfolds must depend on others to guide them.

After all other activities are completed, discuss how drugs are like the balls of yarn. They come at children from all directions, and unless children are determined to avoid them, they may give in. Then discuss how awkward it was to function while impaired, and how drugs always impair people.

✸*D*o-It-Yourself Storybooks

Use this activity to encourage creativity and teamwork. You'll need old magazines, a blank notebook, scissors, glue and a pencil for each team.

Give your group members the opportunity to be instant artists, writers and editors. Divide the group into teams of no more than four. Give each team a stack of magazines, a blank notebook, scissors, glue and a pencil. Give teams each 15 minutes to find at least 10 magazine pictures from which they can create a story. Ask children to glue each picture on a separate notebook page and write a line or two of a story under each picture. Stick with the 15-minute schedule. If children complain, remind them that artists, writers and editors work under strict deadlines.

After the groups have finished their notebooks, get everyone together and have teams take turns reading their stories aloud.

❄*D*on't Get Ripped Off!

This is an interesting and fun way to look at things that can "steal" a person's joy. You'll need three beanbags each labeled "joy," a blindfold and name tags with words such as "worry," "anger," "jealousy," "fear," or "lack of sleep" written on them.

Ask for four volunteers. Blindfold one volunteer and place the beanbags near his or her hand. Have the other three volunteers be "joy thieves" who"ll try to steal the beanbags. Give each thief a name tag labeled "worry," "anger," "jealousy," "fear," "lack of sleep" or anything else that steals joy.

Each thief gets 30 seconds to steal a beanbag. As the first two thieves try, the blindfolded child may only stop the thieves if he or she hears them coming. He or she can't touch the beanbags. To stop the thief, the blindfolded child must listen carefully, then point and yell, "Stop thief!" The blindfolded child has three chances to point and yell at each of the first two thieves. For the third thief, allow the blindfolded child to rest one hand against the remaining beanbag(s). If the child feels a beanbag move, he or she may stop the thief.

Let children take turns playing the different roles.

★Secret Agents

This game teaches thoughtfulness through fun.

For each team you'll need construction paper, markers, a tape recorder and cassette, and transportation.

Before the meeting, decide what missions you'll have children accomplish. Possibilities include: leaving cards on doorsteps of people the group appreciates, visiting someone who's sick, doing something for the church or thanking a school teacher.

If the group is larger than six, divide into teams. Have each child choose a secret-agent name. Give each team a cassette recording that gives details of its mission. Each tape should say what the mission is, how long it'll take and why it's an important mission. Have children leave a construction paper card or note, signed by each secret agent, at each mission site.

Encourage the secret agents to take a few minutes to plan their strategies before going out on the missions. Set a time for secret agents to meet back at the church and report on their missions.

❀ Take a Seat

This is a great way to discover what makes children thankful.

You'll need chairs, a record or cassette player with music, tape and squares of construction paper. Before the meeting, arrange chairs in a circle. Tape a square of construction paper under the seat of every second or third chair.

Have the group play Musical Chairs. Play a song and have children walk around inside the circle of chairs. Then stop the music at random. When the music stops, have each child sit in a chair. Since there are enough chairs for everyone, no one will be "out." But when

everyone is seated, have children each check to see if
there is a construction paper square under the seat of
their chair. Children sitting in chairs with construction
paper squares must each share something they're
thankful for.

✳ *Treasure Hunt*

Here's an old favorite with a new twist.

You'll need 20 small pieces of construction paper.
Before the meeting, write "treasure" words on the pieces
of construction paper, such as the different fruits of the
Spirit, family, friends or the Bible. Hide the papers around
the room or yard.

Form two teams. Allow four minutes for teams to comb
the room or yard and find the hidden treasures. When
the time is up, have teams bring their treasures to you
and read them aloud. The team with the most treasures
wins.

For a variation on this game, make 15 "true" treasures—such as family, friends or the Bible—and five "false"
treasures—such as money, candy or toys. Then form two
teams. Allow four minutes for teams to hunt for the
treasures. When the time is up, have the teams each
separate true treasures from false treasures. Then have
teams turn the true treasures in to you. Each true treasure
turned in is worth 2 points and each false treasure chosen
as a true one takes away 1 point. The team with the most
points wins.

PART 4
Bible-Learning Games

✸ *Bible Baseball*

Studying the Bible or reviewing material can be fun if it's done in creative ways. A good way to study is to play Bible Baseball.

To play Bible Baseball, you'll need chalk, a chalkbaord and prizes.

Bible Baseball is like real baseball in a number of ways: There are two teams, only one person is up at a time and there are three outs. Differences are:

● Children each get two tries to answer a question. On the third "strike," they're out.

● Children don't actually run bases. Instead, they use a baseball diamond and scoreboard drawn on a chalkboard. They draw stick figures at the appropriate bases each time questions are answered correctly.

● There is no real pitcher; the group leader "pitches" each question.

Before the game, write questions and rate them by difficulty. The more difficult the question, the more bases children can run. An example: "For a single, where was Jesus born?" If the "batter" answers "Bethlehem," have him or her draw a stick figure on first base, and call the next batter up.

At the end of the game, award prizes to the winning team. Candy or baseball cards work well.

❄ *Bible-Verse Scramble*

Here's a game that helps children memorize key Bible verses. It works especially well if your group has worked on memorization prior to playing the game.

You'll need 3×5 cards. Choose familiar Bible verses, such as Matthew 28:19. Then write one word of each Bible verse on a separate 3×5 card. For example:

Therefore,	go	make	disciples
of	all	nations	baptizing
them	in	the	name
of	the	Father	and
of	the	Son	and
of	the	Holy	Spirit.

Then make a duplicate of each set of cards. Mix up the cards in each set.

Form two teams. Give a set of face-down cards to each team. Have teams each form circles on opposite sides of the room.

On "go," have teams each throw the cards into the air. Then have children scramble to gather the cards. See which team can put the cards in correct order first. Then play again with another Bible verse.

★ Books of the Bible

This quiet game helps children learn the order of books in the Bible. It works well in confined spaces.

Call several children to the front of the room. Name each one for a book of the Bible. For example, Chris is "Genesis," Beth is "Exodus," Matt is "Leviticus" and Gina is "Numbers." Have "books of the Bible" each stand in the order they appear in the Bible and say their book name. Then have the rest of the group cover their eyes while the books of the Bible scramble. Have children open their eyes and put the books back in order. To make the game more difficult, choose books that aren't consecutive.

❀ Four Gospels

This is a great energizer for the middle of a meeting.

Name each wall of the room for one of the four Gospels. Then when you call out the name of a Gospel, children turn to face that wall. When you call out "good news," children spin around.

There's no winning or losing, just play as long as you want.

✳ *The Fruits of the Spirit*

This fun activity can be done as a field trip or at the church.

You'll need apples, bananas, grapes, oranges, pine-apples, strawberries, pears, peaches, watermelon slices and small towels.

If you use the idea for a field trip, arrange for nine locations as "fruit stops." The locations can be homes, nursing homes, or institutional care centers. Have the group go to each stop and do an assigned "fruity" task. Instruct children to leave the fruit with the people at each stop. Or play the game during a group meeting.

The assignments:

● **Love**—Stand in a line and pass an apple while saying, "Jesus loves you."

● **Joy**—Use bananas for microphones and sing, "I've Got the Joy Down in My Heart."

● **Peace**—Stand in a circle. Give each child some grapes and tell everyone to pass the grapes to the person on the right at the same time while saying, "I'm passing peace to you, my friend."

● **Patience**—Stand in a line and have children pass an orange down the line under their chins. The person passing the orange says, "Patience works. It just takes time."

● **Kindness**—Each child gives a hug, and the group gives a pineapple to someone at the fruit stop or church. Together everyone says, "We're kind when we're giving."

● **Goodness**—Each child picks up 10 pieces of trash and puts it in a trash bin. Give each child a strawberry to eat. Together say, "Because we're good, we can eat something good."

● **Faithfulness**—Walk around in pairs. Have one partner close his or her eyes, carry a pear and say, "I have faith you'll lead me in the right way."

● **Gentleness**—Using small towels as "baby blankets," cradle peaches in your arms like babies. Rock them gently while saying, "Gently, gently we rock you."

● **Self-control**—Stand in a line and pass a slice of watermelon without taking a bite. As the slice of watermelon passes by, have each child say, "I have self-control. I will not eat the watermelon."

When you've finished, read aloud Galatians 5:22-23. Then share watermelon with all of the kids and the people at your fruit stop or church.

✸ *G*oliath Can't Catch Me

Choose one person to be "Goliath." Have that person stand in the middle of the room. Explain that Goliath can't move his or her feet, but can bend over to tag children.

Other players tease Goliath by saying, "Goliath can't catch me," and seeing how close they can get without getting tagged. Each child who's tagged joins Goliath and also tries to tag others without moving his or her feet.

Continue playing until everyone's been tagged.

❄ *Jacob and Rachel*

You'll need one blindfold. Have the group form a circle holding hands. Choose three players to be "Leah," "Rachel" and "Jacob." The characters can be either boys or girls.

Have Leah, Rachel and Jacob go to the center of the circle. Blindfold Jacob and have Leah and Rachel repeatedly call out, "Over here, Jacob!"

Jacob tries to catch Rachel without catching Leah. If Jacob catches Rachel, he chooses someone to take his place and joins the outer circle. If Jacob catches Leah, Leah and Rachel choose children to take their places, and Jacob tries to catch the new Rachel. Children in the outer circle hold hands to keep Leah, Rachel and Jacob in the circle.

★ *The Noah's Ark Show*

Have kids each find a partner. Then have each pair secretly choose an animal from Noah's ark to act out for other teams to guess.

Have one pair go in front of the group and act like its animal, while other pairs try to guess the animal.

When a pair guesses correctly, it goes in front of the group and does its act. If that pair has already done its act, have the two kids choose another pair. This continues until all pairs have been in front of the group. The pair that guesses the most animals correctly wins.

❀ *The Prodigal Son*

You'll need a balloon for each child. Write events from the parable of the prodigal son (Luke 15:11-32) on small slips of paper, one for each balloon. For example:

● Dad divides the property between his two sons.
● Younger son runs away with his money.
● Younger son spends his money.
● Younger son goes broke.
● Younger son decides to come home.
● Dad welcomes the son home.
● Older son gets mad at his dad.
● Dad throws a party because his younger son has come home.

Put one slip of paper into each balloon and blow up the balloons.

Have children form a circle and bat the balloons around. When you yell, "Stop and pop!" have children each grab a balloon, pop it and retrieve the slip of paper.

Then together, have children work out the correct sequence of the parable without looking at the Bible.

When kids work out the correct sequence, read Luke 15:11-32 aloud.

✳ *Scripture Hunt*

Use this fast and furious game to help children burn energy while learning scripture.

You'll need a scripture verse, some paper and lots of imagination. Ahead of time, write a short scripture verse on a piece of paper. Then cut the paper into one- and two-word pieces. Number the pieces of paper and hide them in separate locations in a large room or outside. Make a list of clues, numbered so each clue matches the number of the hidden word. For example, if word #1 is hidden in a bush, its clue could be: "I'm bushed" or

"You'll be bushed if you find me."

Divide your group into two teams and give each team a clue list. Give teams three minutes to find as many words as they can. Then have them try to figure out the scripture verse from the words they've found.

The first team to guess the verse correctly wins.

✳*Signs* of the Times

Before the game, write names of significant people in the Old and New Testaments on separate 3×5 cards. Make two sets of identical 12 cards with a mixture of Old and New Testament names.

Form two teams of equal size. Designate one team A and the other team B. Give each team a set of cards. Have teams each look at their cards one at a time and agree whether the person is in the Old or New Testament. Then have the team send a runner to that station. (See diagram below.)

The team in a set amount of time with the most correct choices wins.

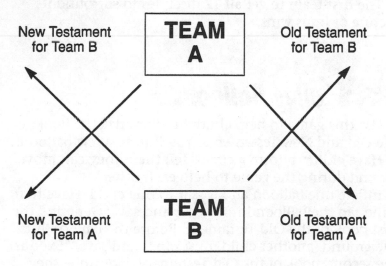

New Testament
for Team B

**TEAM
A**

Old Testament
for Team B

New Testament
for Team A

**TEAM
B**

Old Testament
for Team A

❄ *The Twelve Disciples*

To help children learn the disciples' names, try this competitive team game.

Before the meeting, write the 12 disciples' names on 12 separate 3×5 cards. Make a duplicate set. According to Matthew 10:2-4, the disciples' names were: Simon Peter, Andrew, John, James son of Zebedee, Philip, Bartholomew, Thomas, Matthew, James son of Alphaeus, Thaddaeus, Simon the Zealot and Judas Iscariot. Find two pictures of Jesus and tape them to the wall.

To play, form two equal teams. Assign a picture of Jesus to each team. Tell the teams you'll ask questions about the Bible. Flip a coin to see which team will answer the first question; then take turns. Ask questions such as: "How many books are in the New Testament?" and "Who got thrown into the lion's den?"

Each time a team answers correctly, give it a 3×5 card with a disciple's name to tape to the wall near the picture of Jesus. When a team answers a question incorrectly, remove one of the 3×5 cards from near that team's picture of Jesus.

The first team to get all 12 disciples to surround its picture of Jesus wins.

☆ *Volley Balloons*

Use this game to help children memorize the books of the Old and New Testaments. You'll need a few balloons.

Have children form a circle. Tell them they can move around during the game to help each other.

Inflate one balloon and toss it to one child. Have that child tap the balloon into the air and say, "Genesis," the first book of the Old Testament. Before the balloon hits the ground, another child must tap it and says, "Exodus," the second book of the Old Testament. Continue the game until the books of the Old Testament are named in the correct order. The object of the game is to keep a balloon airborne throughout the entire listing of the Old Testament. Then do the New Testament books.

For variety, use other topics with this game, such as the disciples' names, the fruits of the Spirit and the words of scripture verses such as John 3:16.

❀ *W*et Winners

This is a great game for a hot, summer day.

You'll need a water pistol. Have children sit in a circle. Choose one player to be "It," and to stand in the center of circle with the water pistol.

Have "It" think of someone or something from the Bible and give children a category to guess from. For example, if "It" is thinking of Daniel, "It" would say, "Someone in the Old Testament." Then have "It" walk around the inside of the circle while each child guesses. The child who guesses correctly gets a wet shot from the water pistol. That child becomes the new "It."

PART 5
Energy Burners

✳*A*dam and the Animals

Choose one child to be "Adam." Have him or her stand at one end of the room. (See diagram.) Have the rest of the group stand together behind a masking-tape line at the other end of the room. This is "home."

Have the group choose one animal from God's creation. Then have children walk up to Adam and dance around him acting like that animal. Have Adam try to guess the name of the animal. As soon as Adam guesses correctly, have all the "animals" run home while Adam tries to catch one.

If an animal is caught, he or she becomes Adam for the next round. If no one is caught, the same person is Adam.

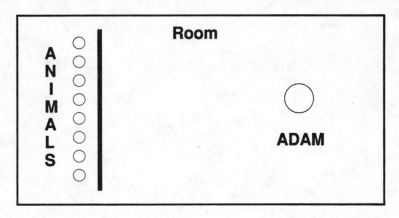

✸*B*arley Field

A version of this game was played by children in the fields of Israel after harvest many years ago.

Play this game in a long narrow area such as a driveway, sidewalk or hallway. Or mark an outside area with chalk dust. Divide the area into three sections. The center section is the barley field.

Two players are "It." They link arms and guard the barley field. Other players find partners and link arms. Each pair chooses one of the end sections as home base.

On a given signal, such as a whistle blow, players from the two end sections leave home base, enter the barley field, kneel, then return to home base. The guards of the barley field try to tag pairs in the field. Each pair tagged is frozen and must remain where tagged. The game leader watches the game and repeats the signal to enter the barley field as needed. The game ends when only one pair remains untagged. The winning pair becomes "It" and the game starts over.

❄ *B*lind Shoe-Search

This "sole" game helps children loosen up and have fun.

You'll need a blindfold for each child. Have children form a circle. Then ask them to take off their shoes and toss them in the middle. Mix up the shoes.

Blindfold each player. Then mix up the shoes again. On "go," have children try to figure out which shoes are theirs. Encourage them to try on different shoes. When children think they've found their own shoes, have them put on both shoes.

Play until everyone is wearing a pair of shoes. Then have children take off their blindfolds to see who has matching shoes and who doesn't!

★Bus

This highly active game is a blast to play.

Line up chairs like seats in a bus. (See diagram.) You'll need enough chairs for the number of people in the group—minus two. Choose one child to be the "chaser" and another to be the "chasee." Have the chaser and chasee stand on either side of the chairs. Have the rest of the children sit in the bus seats. As children sit down, have them each introduce themselves and ask their fellow passenger, "If you could visit anywhere in the world, where would you go, and why?"

The chaser and chasee begin running around the outside perimeter of the seats. The chaser tries to tag the chasee. The chasee, however, can slide into any seat by pushing the child in that seat into the next seat. The person forced out of that seat then becomes the chasee. The chaser then pursues the new chasee. If the chaser tags the chasee, the roles reverse.

After the game has progressed for a while, yell, "I smell smoke!" Then have children change seats in a "fruit-basket-upset" manner. Make sure everyone moves, so the chaser and chasee can get seats and rest. The last two children left standing become the new chaser and chasee. Flip a coin to see which becomes the chaser or the chasee, and start the game again.

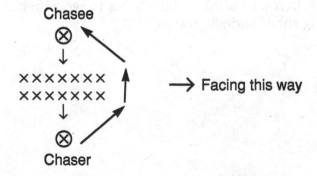

❀ *Chicken*

Chicken is a Hopscotch-type game played in China.

Have players each remove one shoe. Place the shoes in a straight line about one foot apart.

The first player hops on his or her shoed foot over each of the shoes in the line. When the player gets to the last shoe, he or she kicks that shoe out of line, then turns and hops back over the remaining shoes. If the player puts both feet on the ground at any time, a second player takes over at that place. The game continues in the same manner until all the shoes are kicked out of place. When all the shoes are kicked out of place, line them up again so everyone gets a turn.

✳ *Circle Tag*

Here's an active game that requires cooperation.

You'll need one bandanna. Choose one child to be "It." Have the rest of the group form a circle holding hands. Stick the bandanna in the hip pocket of one of the players.

"It" runs around the outside of the circle trying to grab the bandanna while the circle turns either clockwise or counterclockwise trying to save the bandanna. If the bandanna is caught, "It" joins the circle and a new "It" is chosen.

If you have a large group, try the game with two bandannas on two different players.

✳*Dodge Towel*

This game helps a restless group burn excess energy.

You'll need an old towel, folded and rolled so it's 12 to 18 inches long. Wrap it in a couple of places with strong tape to hold it in a roll. If you have a very large group, prepare two or three towels.

The object of the game is to throw the towel and hit someone with it. Any child who's hit is out and must stand on the sidelines until the next game. There are no teams in this game—the last child left wins.

The game is played in a room or gym depending on the size of your group. To begin the game, everyone stands against the wall with the towel on the floor in the center of the room. On "go," everybody tries to get the towel and throw it at others while avoiding being hit themselves. The person who has the towel may take only two steps, but all others may run around as much as they please.

As the game progresses, and fewer children remain in the game, the room may need to be divided in half so the remaining players will have less space to run in.

The last child wins and a new game begins.

❄ *Grab-Base Tag*

Select two children to play Tag. Have the child whose birthday is closest to today's date be the "chaser," and the child whose birthday is next closest to today be the "chasee." Have the other children form pairs and hold hands. If you have an uneven number of children, have an adult play. Have the pairs scatter over the playing area. They're the "bases."

The bases don't move as the chaser tries to tag the chasee, but they hold out their free hands, waiting to be grabbed. To get "on base" and avoid being tagged, the chasee grabs a free hand of one of the bases. Then the person at the other end of the pair becomes the chasee and runs away from the chaser. When the chaser tags the chasee, the chasee becomes the new chaser. The old chaser is allowed to grab a base, and another child is the new chasee.

If your group is large enough and you want to make the chase more challenging, reduce the number of bases. To do this, stop the game every few minutes and form bases of three, then four, then five people. As the bases get larger, one can be a different size than the others.

★ *The Raj*

This old game was once a contact sport with guards forcefully saving the Raj. Try this less-violent version.

Choose one child to be the "Raj" and two children to be the "bodyguards." The rest of the players become members of the "rabble." Set up two markers about 25 feet apart.

The Raj tries to walk from one marker to the other by putting the heel of one foot to the toe of the other, traveling heel to toe the whole distance. Members of the rabble try to tag the Raj. The bodyguards try to prevent this by circling the Raj and trying to tag the rabble rouser. The bodyguards must not leave the Raj to chase anyone from the rabble; they must circle the Raj at all times.

If the Raj is tagged by one of the rabble, the tagger becomes the Raj. If a bodyguard tags one of the rabble, that person must sit down and count to 50 before rejoining the game. If the Raj makes it to the marker without being tagged, a new Raj and new bodyguards are chosen for the return trip.

❀ *R*ounder

Choose this crazy circle game when you want to work off some energy.

One child is "It." The rest of the children sit in a close circle with their backs to the center of the circle. They link arms so all are joined in an inside-out circle. "It" walks around the outside of the circle and taps one child on the foot. "It" immediately starts to count to 25. The circle must stand up, circle to the left one complete revolution and sit down without unlinking arms before "It" counts to 25. If the circle is successful "It" continues around the circle and taps another player on the foot. If "It" finishes counting before the circle sits down, he or she changes places with the child tapped. If you're playing with more than 10 players, have "It" count to a higher number.

✳ Runaway Gingerbread Cookies

Tell the children you baked some gingerbread cookies for everyone to eat, but the cookies ran away to the church sanctuary.

Have the children go to the sanctuary to look for the cookies. Have a church staff person waiting in the sanctuary with another clue about where the cookies ran next. Have children keep following clues until they meet all the church staff people and also see parts of the church they may have never seen (such as the janitor's closet or behind the pulpit). Have the cookies ready to eat at a final destination.

✴ Vine and Fig Tree

Play this ancient game either indoors or outdoors.

Each player chooses a base such as a tree or a chair. At the blow of a whistle or other signal, all players leave their bases and try to tag other players. After a short interval, another signal is given. All kids return to their bases except those tagged. Tagged kids each go to the base of the person who tagged them. At another signal, all children again leave their bases and try to tag others. Continue until everyone's on one or two teams.

PART 6
Group Fun

❄*A*nimal Flashcards

Children will need to be quick to keep up in this game.

For each player, you'll need a set of 10 animal cards. All sets must be identical. These can be made by gluing animal pictures or writing animal names on 3×5 cards.

Players each shuffle their own set of cards and lay them face down on the table. The first two players turn up the top cards of their decks at the same time. If the cards match, the first player to call out the name of the animal on the cards wins both cards. If the cards don't match, they try again. When the decks are gone, the player with the most cards wins.

The winner from the first two players then plays against a third player and so on around the circle. When players have gone through all the cards, they reshuffle them and keep playing. The child with the most cards at the end of the game wins.

✫*C*an You Jive Like This?

Try this rhythm game for some silly fun.

Form a circle with the leader in the middle. The leader starts the game by saying, "Can you jive like this?" and doing an action, such as touching an elbow to a knee. The group answers, "I can jive like that," and copies the action. Repeat the process twice with different actions. After the third action, the leader joins the circle and the circle moves counterclockwise snapping fingers and "truckin' " to the beat as they chant:

"I can jive like that, I can boogie down,
I can shake my shoulders and go to town."

The leader moves back into the center of the circle and starts again, or a new leader may be chosen. Encourage several children to take turns leading. The game should move rapidly with no breaks in the action.

❀*D*inosaur-Egg Hunt

Dinosaurs are big among children of any age. This fun game turns fruit into "dinosaur eggs" for a scavenger hunt. The game may be played outside by one group, individuals or teams.

You'll need various kinds of fruit that might pass for dinosaur eggs, such as watermelons, cantaloupes, grapefruits and oranges.

Before the group arrives, hide the dinosaur eggs among leaves, weeds, tall grasses or pine needles.

When the group arrives, explain that dinosaurs have been seen in the area and the group has been asked to look for the eggs. Tell children it's very important that they find the eggs before they hatch, or there'll be a dinosaur population explosion. Describe the eggs' colors, sizes and shapes.

Send the children out to look for the eggs. Have them bring the eggs back to a central location. After one egg is found, the idea will catch on. Points can be assigned for each type of egg.

After all of the eggs are found, have the group eat the dinosaur eggs or make a dinosaur "egg salad."

✳*E*lastic Circle

This activity provides a good stretch in the middle of a meeting.

Have children hold hands in a circle and pretend to form an elastic band. Have the circle stretch out as far as possible, then go inward, then stretch out again until the circle breaks. Then have children form small elastic bands of two or three.

✳*Fractured Matches*

Form two teams. Give each child a piece of paper and a marker. Designate one team to be the "adjectives" and the other team to be the "nouns."

Have children each write one word on their piece of paper from their team's category. For example, adjective team members might write "striped," "pink" or "ugly." Children in the noun group might write "zebra," "car" or "movie star."

Have the nouns form a circle and hold their pieces of paper so everyone can read what they wrote. Have the adjectives form a circle inside the noun circle and also hold up what they wrote.

Play music. Have the nouns walk clockwise and the adjectives walk counterclockwise. When the music stops, have adjective children each pair up with the noun person closest to them. Then have each pair read their words together. For example, "striped car," "pink zebra" or "ugly movie star." Then play the music again and have the circles move until the music stops. Play several times to hear many different crazy combinations.

❄*Fun for the Frugal*

Check out these games that children love. They're easy to set up and inexpensive. They can be used for vacation Bible school, camps or fellowship meetings.

● **Ring the Prize**—Pound a nail in the middle of a block of wood so the nail sticks up. Cut out the centers of plastic coffee-can covers. Have children toss them over the nails for prizes.

● **Candy Game**—Buy lots of suckers. Color the tips of about $1/5$ of them. Poke holes in a box top and stand the suckers up with the tips inside the holes so they aren't showing. Have children each select a sucker. Award prizes to children who choose suckers with colored tips.

● **Bowling**—Set up a "bowling alley" using toy bowling pins and a softball. Use a table with boards along the sides so the softball won't roll away. If children roll a strike, they'll receive a first prize. If they roll a spare, they'll get a second prize.

● **Fish**—Place a tall sheet of plywood against a table. Make fishing poles from long sticks and string, using paper clips as hooks. Have children each drop their line over the plywood and have someone hook a prize on it.

● **Football Through the Tire**—Hang some old tires from sturdy tree limbs. Have children throw footballs through the tires for prizes.

● **Ball in the Basket**—Have children throw a ball into a clothes basket. Or challenge children to toss the ball through a hoop and into the basket.

● **Boat Game**—With waterproof markers, mark numbers on the bottoms of some inexpensive toy boats. Place the boats in a pan of water. Have children each select a boat. The number on the boat they pull out indicates what prize they win.

● **Feed the Cartoon Character**—Paint a cartoon character on a sheet of plywood. Cut out the mouth. Have children each throw a ball or a beanbag into its mouth for a prize.

Most novelty stores have small prizes for a few cents each. Or bulk prizes can be ordered through novelty companies. Distributors often have coloring books, storybooks and puzzles they'll donate.

★ *Guess What's Gross*

This activity always gets lots of laughs as children get "in touch" with some gross items.

You'll need whatever items you can think of that feel gross. See the list for a few ideas.

Ask for five volunteers to be on a panel. Have the volunteers sit in front of the group at a table. Blindfold them. Then have each child feel the items one at a time using touch only. The child who guesses the most items correctly wins.

Some examples:
- wet pickles;
- wet noodles;
- ketchup;
- olives;
- applesauce;
- relish;
- raw chicken livers; or
- water.

❀ *Green Light Go!*

This game gets a group together.

You'll need three blankets, towels or sheets—one red, one yellow and one green. Lay the blankets side by side on the ground. Tell kids the colors represent a traffic light.

Have all the children stand on the yellow (middle) blanket. When you shout another color, have the children quickly move to the appropriate blanket. The last child to get both feet on the correct blanket is eliminated from the game.

To make the game more challenging, occasionally call out the color on which the children are already standing. Anyone who steps off that blanket is eliminated.

For a change of pace, call out "traffic accident" and have everyone vacate all blankets. The last child to get off is eliminated.

Keep the pace quick and vary the colors called. The winner is the last person to remain in the traffic light.

✳ *"I" Game*

This activity helps children focus on others rather than themselves. You'll need 10 dried beans for each child.

As children arrive, give them each 10 beans. Have children mingle and talk about their previous week. Whenever someone says "I," any listener who catches it gets a bean. The person with the most beans after five minutes wins.

✸*In the Whale's Mouth*

Have children count off by threes. Have all the ones become "whales" and spread throughout the room, moving their arms like whales' mouths.

Have the twos each find a whale and stand inside its mouth, so each one is hugging a two.

Then have the threes "swim" around the room, mimicking a swimming stroke and waiting for an empty whale's mouth to stand in.

When you yell, "Switch," all twos leave the whales' mouths and compete with the threes to quickly swim inside another whale's mouth. Continue playing the game by yelling "Switch!"

❄*M*ousie

Games similar to this were played in the Victorian era. It plays best in a room with lots of furniture.

Choose one child to be the "mother mouse" and another to be the "owl." Other players are "baby mice."

The mother mouse leads the baby mice, crawling under chairs and around tables. The babies must follow her route exactly. When all the babies are following the mother, signal the owl to start. The owl also follows the path of the mother exactly, trying to catch the babies. If the owl can crawl fast enough, he or she can catch the last baby in line. Any time after the owl starts, the mother mouse can stand and run back to the starting place. The baby mice stand and follow her and the owl chases them. When the owl catches a baby, either crawling or running, the captured baby becomes the owl and the owl becomes the mother mouse for the next game.

★ Musical Hugs

Count how many children are present. If you have an odd number, great. If you have an even number, ask an adult volunteer to join the game.

Have children jog around the room to music. When the music stops, have each child hug the person closest to him or her. The person left out must choose one other person to sit out with him or her. Then start the game again. Play until one child is left.

Award the winner by having him or her stand in the middle of the group for a big group hug!

❀ Numbers Hugs

Choose one person to be "It." Have the rest of the children spread out around the room. Then have "It" call out numbers between two and the number of children playing.

As soon as the number is called, have children run and form a group hug with that many people. For example, if "three" is called, have groups of three children hug together. Of those left out from each hug, choose one person to be "It."

✳ *P*atti-knees

Everyone works together to make this game a success.

You'll need a record or tape player and some music with a strong beat.

Seat everyone in a circle on the floor with legs crossed and close together so knees are touching. Put your hands on your neighbor's knees on each side of you. Have your neighbors cross their arms over yours to put their hands on your knees. Have children continue the pattern around the circle.

Now, start with your right hand and pat the knee your hand is on. Continue clockwise around the circle, having children each pat one knee at a time. For example, if you're sitting between Kelly and Stacy, you'll pat Stacy's left knee with your right hand. Then Stacy will pat your right knee with her left hand. Then Kelly will pat your left knee with her right hand, and you'll pat Kelly's right knee with your left hand.

When children can continue this around the circle, try the pats to the beat of the music. When anyone makes a mistake, reverse the direction of the pats.

✸ *S*howerball

This game combines the best of basketball and water balloons.

You'll need to prepare some water balloons.

Line up the group from tallest to shortest and count off by fours. Ones and fours make one team, and twos and threes make the other team. Explain that the game is played and scored just like basketball. But because water balloons are used instead of a ball, certain modifications to the rules are necessary:

● The balloon can't be dribbled. It must be passed from player to player. No player may run with the balloon.

● If a balloon breaks in play, a new one is put into play by the opposing team.

● To count as a score, the balloon must pass through the hoop before it breaks.

● Intentional or rough physical contact between players is a foul, and the balloon goes to the other team. There are no foul shots.

● If the boys tend to leave the girls out of the game, a rule can be added that requires boys to pass the balloon to girls and girls to pass the balloon to boys.

The game ends at a preset time or score or when the supply of balloons is exhausted.

Have kids clean up the mess at the end of the game.

❄ *Sound-Effects Game*

This game is just for fun and doesn't involve competition.

Form teams of no more than four. One at a time, give teams each a sound to make. Players can use only their voices and their bodies (slapping knees, clapping, stomping feet) to produce the given sounds. Here are some "sound" ideas:

● fans of a losing football team;
● chickens at feeding time;
● preschoolers at a fast-food restaurant;
● a stock-car race;
● the percussion section of a marching band;
● thoroughbred horses in a race;
● a passenger train at full speed;
● tap dancers in a chorus line;
● popcorn popping; or
● a clock shop at noon.

☆ Soup's On

This game later becomes a snack.

You'll need masking tape, a large soup pot, a ladle, water, a can opener, cups, spoons and access to a stove. Ask children each to bring a can of their favorite condensed soup to the meeting. Have a couple of extra cans available for anyone who forgets.

On a tile or smooth concrete floor, put a strip of masking tape for the starting line. Eight feet from that strip, put another strip of masking tape about 4 feet long. Five inches beyond that strip, put another 4-foot strip. Put a fourth 4-foot strip another 5 inches away.

Have the children each stand behind the starting line and take turns rolling their can of soup. Cans that stop between the second and third strips are worth 10 points. Cans that stop between the third and fourth strips are worth 20 points. Cans that pass the fourth strip are worth 5 points. The scoring is collective. Everyone rolls and all the points are added into one score. If a can stops in the first 10-point spot, children can try to nudge it into the 20-point spot with another can to improve the score.

When children are tired of playing, have them open their cans and put all the soup in the pot with equal amounts of water. Heat it to boiling and serve this one-of-a-kind soup for your snack.

❀ Watch Out Down Under

Choose one person to be "It." Have the rest of the group form a circle around "It." Have children in the circle stand with their feet spread a shoulder's width apart, touching the next player's feet.

Then have "It" stand in the center of the circle with a ball. Have him or her try to roll the ball out of the circle between someone's legs. The ball can't leave the ground, and players can only use their hands to stop the ball. They can't move their feet. When someone lets the ball out of the circle between his or her legs, he or she becomes the next "It."

✳ Zoo Love

Children love to go on field trips to the zoo. Here's an idea for helping them learn what animals love.

You'll need a list of questions and a pencil for each team.

Take the group to your local zoo and divide into teams of no more than four. Give each team a list of zoo-love questions. Ask teams to meet at a designated spot and time. (You may want to check with the zoo ahead of time to make sure an animal fits each question.)

The zoo-love questions:

● Which animal would you love to hold?
● Which animal would you love to kiss?
● Which animal loves to climb trees?
● Which animal loves the beach?
● Which animal would you love to hug?
● Which animal loves the forest?
● Which animal loves to run?
● Which animal loves to be cold?
● Which animal loves dirt?
● Which animal loves the sky?

● Which animal loves mountains?
● Which animal loves water?
● Which animal loves to sleep?
● Which youth leader loves to eat?
The winners are the children who have the most fun!

PART 7
Relays

✸*B*arefoot Relay

For this goofy variation of the common relay, you'll need a few marbles. Form equal teams. Have kids each take off their shoes and socks. Designate a goal about 20 feet away.

Have teams each form a single line. Give the first player of each team a marble to put between his or her toes. On "go," have children each hobble to the goal and back without losing control of the marble. If the child loses control of the marble, he or she must run back to the starting line and begin again.

When a child successfully hobbles to the designated point and back without losing control of the marble, he or she tags the next child and gives that child the marble. The first team to finish wins.

❄*C*otton-Ball Relay

This easy, indoor relay race involves two or more teams.

For each team, you'll need a spoon, a piece of construction paper or posterboard, a goal marked on the floor, and a large bowl filled with cotton balls.

Give the first child on each team a spoon and piece of construction paper or posterboard. The race begins as the first player on each team uses the spoon to capture a cotton ball from the bowl. He or she holds the spoon with the cotton ball in it in one hand, and the paper in the other hand. The player carries the cotton ball in the spoon across the room and drops it on the goal on the floor. Then using the paper as a fan, the player fans the cotton ball along as he or she walks back to the team. Then the child hands the spoon and the paper to the next player and the relay continues.

A variation is to have a leader stand near the goals and to call out different things for the players to do while carrying or fanning the cotton ball, such as hop on one foot, walk backward, crawl, skip or walk sideways.

☆Daddy-Long-Legs Relay

This energy releaser requires kids to work together. You'll need a two-foot length of rope for each person.

This is a long version of the traditional three-legged race. Form equal teams of four to seven people. Each team stands side by side behind a designated starting line. Hand each child a length of rope. Have children each tie their right ankle to the left ankle of the person on their right. All teammates should be tied to each other. Have each team coordinate which ankle pairs should step forward first. When all teams are ready, have them race to a goal and back.

If your group has less than eight children, form one daddy-long-legs team and race the clock. Run several races and see if faster times can be achieved.

❀ *H*oppin' Poppin' Relay

For sheer enjoyment of racing and popcorn, try this one.

You'll need a paper plate for each person, popcorn and three buckets.

Form two teams. Have team members line up. Put a bucket of popcorn at the center of a designated goal line and an empty bucket at the head of each team line. Give each child a paper plate. On "go," have the first relay runner on each team hop to the goal, grab a handful of popcorn, put it on the paper plate and hop back. Have him or her empty the popcorn into the team bucket. Give each team member a turn. The winner is the team with the most popcorn at the end of the game.

Then comes the fun part: eating the popcorn.

✳*Ice* Cream-Sundae Relay

What child doesn't like ice cream? For every four children, you'll need a pint of ice cream, chocolate syrup, nuts and spoons.

Form teams of four players each. Give the first person in each team one pint of ice cream and a spoon. Give the second person in each team chocolate syrup. Give the third person some nuts. The fourth person will eat.

On "go," the first person scoops some ice cream and gives the spoon to the second person who adds chocolate syrup to it. Then the second person gives the spoon to the third person, who adds nuts and feeds the fourth person.

After the fourth person swallows the ice cream, he or she runs to the start of the line, grabs a new spoon, scoops ice cream from the pint and starts it down the line again as all the team members shift one position.

The first team to eat its entire pint of ice cream wins.

✸*M*asterpiece Relay

This relay helps build teamwork skills and is also just plain fun.

You'll need crayons, masking tape and large pieces of paper.

Form teams of no more than five, and give each team a set of crayons. A short distance from the teams, tape large pieces of paper to a table or wall. You may want to put newspaper on the wall around each paper. On each large piece of paper, write a caption describing a picture to draw. Each team should have the same description. Make the description complex enough so each team member will have at least one item to draw. For example: (1) A man in blue jeans (2) sits in a sailboat (3) drinking cola (4) while reading a book (5) on a choppy ocean.

In relay style, have one team member race to the canvas, draw one of the descriptions and check off what he or she has drawn. Have that child run back and tag the next person who continues the picture. The first team to successfully complete its masterpiece wins.

Other masterpiece ideas include:

● (1) On the green chalkboard (2) the teacher with gray hair (3) and the student wearing orange and blue ribbons (4) did math problems.

● (1) The baby in the cradle (2) who held a bottle of grape juice in one hand (3) and a red-striped rattle in the other (4) wore a pink and blue baby bonnet (5) and was crying as loudly as she could.

❄*P*aper-Cup Relay

Are your children all wet? They will be after this wild relay.

You'll need a paper cup for each child.

Form two teams. Have teams each stand in a straight line. Give each team member a small paper cup to hold with his or her teeth. Fill the first child's cup on each team with water. Have each player pour water from his or her cup into the next person's cup using his or her teeth. No hands are allowed.

The team with the most water in the last person's cup wins.

☆*Peanut-Scoop Relay*

Here's a fun relay that can be done either indoors or out.

You'll need plenty of unshelled peanuts, a bowl and two jars of equal size.

Form two equal teams. About 20 feet away, set two jars of equal size with the lids off. Have team members stand in a straight line. Place a bowl of peanuts next to the first person on each team.

On "go," have the first person on each team scoop up as many peanuts as he or she can hold with only one hand. Players each must keep the other hand behind their back with their palm open.

One at a time, have players run to their jar and dump in the peanuts. They can't pick up any dropped peanuts. Then have the players run back and tag the next teammate who does the same. When all children have taken a turn, count the peanuts in each jar and declare a winner.

❀*Spelling-Blocks Relay*

Here's another fun idea for relay team competition.

You'll need a set of alphabet blocks for each team. Borrow them from your church nursery, or purchase them from a local toy or discount store.

Form equal teams. Line up teams behind a starting line. Place a pile of alphabet blocks on the floor at the opposite end of the room for each team. Give teams a word to spell with the blocks. Make sure beforehand that each pile of blocks has all the letters you need for the particular word or phrase you want children to spell. On "go," the first child on each team runs to the team's pile of blocks and finds the first letter of the word the team must spell. He or she runs that block back to the team.

The second teammate runs to the block pile and finds the second letter. The first team to spell the word wins. Then have children return all the blocks to their respective piles and move on to a new word.

✳ Surprise-Stunt Relay

This relay will keep children on their toes because they won't know what they need to do next. The materials you'll need will depend on the activities you choose.

Form teams of equal size. Fill one paper bag for each team with plastic bags that include written instructions and materials for each team member to do a stunt. Some ideas:

● Eat a cracker. Then whistle a verse of "Amazing Grace."

● Tie a yarn ankle bracelet around a teammate's ankle.

● Blow up a balloon. Tie it. Then sit on it and pop it.

● On a teammate's cheek, use lipstick to draw a heart and color it in.

● Place a peanut between your knees and hop back to your team without losing the peanut.

Place the paper bags, with plastic bags inside, about 20 feet away from the teams. On "go," have the first child from each team run to the paper bag, pull out one plastic bag, perform the stunt and run back to tag the second child in line.

The first team to successfully complete all the stunts is the winner.

Creative Resources for Your Children's Ministry

CHILDREN'S MINISTRY CLIP ART

By Mary Lynn Ulrich

Add pizazz and style to your ministry with **Children's Ministry Clip Art**. Use these lively illustrations in newsletters, fliers, letters and on bulletin boards—anywhere you need to grab kid's—and parent's—attention.

With this creative art, you can ...

- design fabulous fliers and handouts for meetings on dozens of topics;
- announce upcoming events with zany, attention-getting calendars; and
- promote specific children's ministry programs.

This giant collection of clip art will add a professional touch to your children's ministry. It's as easy as 1-2-3.

    1-Choose your art   2-Cut it out   3-Paste it down

and your publicity is ready to go!

ISBN 1-55945-018-5 $14.95

QUICK GROUP DEVOTIONS FOR CHILDREN'S MINISTRY

From the editors of Group Books

Discover quick, fun devotions for your children's ministry.

You'll get 52 easy, meaningful ideas. Each devotion deepens kids' faith while requiring little or no personal planning time. Each devotion comes complete with Bible passage, fun learning activity, discussion questions, and closing prayer. These devotions apply God's Word to younger kids' lives, helping them explore important issues ...

- Love
- Worry
- Peer pressure
- Faith
- Honesty
- Friendship

... and many more, including devotions for New Year's Day, Valentines Day, Christmas and other special occasions.

ISBN 1-55945-004-5 $7.95

Practical Programming for Your Children's Ministry

UPPER-ELEMENTARY MEETINGS

From the editors of Group Books

Build faith in upper-elementary kids! You'll discover 20 well-planned meetings on a variety of topics—all designed specifically to build faith in upper-elementary kids. You'll save tons of planning time as you teach powerful Christian lessons such as . . .

- Being a child of God
- Helping the hungry
- What's great about parents
- God's will
- Temptation
- What is faith?

All step-by-step meeting plans come complete with crowd-breakers, Bible studies and devotions. Plus, you'll cut preparation time with loads of creative handouts you can photocopy. Your kids will love the action built into each program. And you'll get solid help dealing with the tough issues they now face . . .

- Divorce
- Self-Image
- Peer pressure
- Drugs
- Sexuality

. . . and more.

ISBN 0-931529-86-7 $11.95